MW00700891

THIS NOTEBOOK BELONGS TO:

NAME • _____

CONTACT • _____

EMAIL • _____

Recipe

Prep Time:

Cook Time:

Difficulty: ○ ○ ○ ○ ○

Serves:　1　2　3　4　5　6　7　8　9　+

Pleasure: ○ ○ ○ ○ ○

Ingredients

Directions

Notes

Recipe

Prep Time:

Cook Time:

Difficulty: ○ ○ ○ ○ ○

Serves: 1   2   3   4   5   6   7   8   9   +

Pleasure: ○ ○ ○ ○ ○

Ingredients

_____ _____

_____ _____

_____ _____

_____ _____

_____ _____

_____ _____

Directions

_____

_____

_____

_____

_____

_____

_____

_____

_____

_____

Notes

_____

_____

_____

_____

B C D E F G H I J K L M N O P Q R S T U V W X Y Z

Recipe

Prep Time:

Cook Time:

Difficulty: ○ ○ ○ ○ ○

Serves: 1 2 3 4 5 6 7 8 9 +

Pleasure: ○ ○ ○ ○ ○

Ingredients

Directions

Notes

Recipe

Prep Time:	Cook Time:	Difficulty: ○ ○ ○ ○ ○

Serves: 1   2   3   4   5   6   7   8   9   +   Pleasure: ○ ○ ○ ○ ○

Ingredients

_____   _____

_____   _____

_____   _____

_____   _____

_____   _____

_____   _____

Directions

_____

_____

_____

_____

_____

_____

_____

_____

_____

_____

_____

Notes

_____

_____

_____

_____

Recipe

Prep Time:

Cook Time:

Difficulty: ○ ○ ○ ○ ○

Serves: 1   2   3   4   5   6   7   8   9   +

Pleasure: ○ ○ ○ ○ ○

Ingredients

Directions

Notes

Recipe

Prep Time:

Cook Time:

Difficulty: ○ ○ ○ ○ ○

Serves: 1   2   3   4   5   6   7   8   9   +

Pleasure: ○ ○ ○ ○ ○

Ingredients

Directions

Notes

Recipe

Prep Time:

Cook Time:

Difficulty: ○ ○ ○ ○ ○

Serves: 1   2   3   4   5   6   7   8   9   +

Pleasure: ○ ○ ○ ○ ○

Ingredients

Directions

Notes

Recipe

Prep Time:

Cook Time:

Difficulty: ○ ○ ○ ○ ○

Serves: 1   2   3   4   5   6   7   8   9   +

Pleasure: ○ ○ ○ ○ ○

Ingredients

_____   _____

_____   _____

_____   _____

_____   _____

_____   _____

_____   _____

Directions

_____

_____

_____

_____

_____

_____

_____

_____

_____

_____

Notes

_____

_____

_____

_____

Recipe

Prep Time:

Cook Time:

Difficulty: ○ ○ ○ ○ ○

Serves: 1   2   3   4   5   6   7   8   9   +

Pleasure: ○ ○ ○ ○ ○

Ingredients

Directions

Notes

Recipe

Prep Time:	Cook Time:	Difficulty: ○ ○ ○ ○ ○
Serves: 1 2 3 4 5 6 7 8 9 +		Pleasure: ○ ○ ○ ○ ○

Ingredients

_____   _____

_____   _____

_____   _____

_____   _____

_____   _____

_____   _____

Directions

_____

_____

_____

_____

_____

_____

_____

_____

_____

_____

Notes

_____

_____

_____

_____

Recipe

B

| Prep Time: | Cook Time: | Difficulty: ○ ○ ○ ○ ○ |
| Serves: 1 2 3 4 5 6 7 8 9 + | | Pleasure: ○ ○ ○ ○ ○ |

Ingredients

Directions

Notes

Recipe

Prep Time:

Cook Time:

Difficulty: ○ ○ ○ ○ ○

Serves: 1   2   3   4   5   6   7   8   9   +

Pleasure: ○ ○ ○ ○ ○

Ingredients

Directions

Notes

Recipe

Prep Time:

Cook Time:

Difficulty: ○ ○ ○ ○ ○

Serves: 1   2   3   4   5   6   7   8   9   +

Pleasure: ○ ○ ○ ○ ○

Ingredients

Directions

Notes

Recipe

| Prep Time: | Cook Time: | Difficulty: ○ ○ ○ ○ ○ |

Serves: 1 2 3 4 5 6 7 8 9 +   Pleasure: ○ ○ ○ ○ ○

Ingredients

_____   _____
_____   _____
_____   _____
_____   _____
_____   _____
_____   _____

Directions

_____
_____
_____
_____
_____
_____
_____
_____
_____
_____
_____

Notes

_____
_____
_____
_____

Recipe

Prep Time:

Cook Time:

Difficulty: ○ ○ ○ ○ ○

Serves: 1   2   3   4   5   6   7   8   9   +

Pleasure: ○ ○ ○ ○ ○

Ingredients

Directions

Notes

Recipe

Prep Time:

Cook Time:

Difficulty: ○ ○ ○ ○ ○

Serves: 1 2 3 4 5 6 7 8 9 +

Pleasure: ○ ○ ○ ○ ○

Ingredients

Directions

Notes

Recipe

Prep Time:

Cook Time:

Difficulty: ○ ○ ○ ○ ○

Serves: 1   2   3   4   5   6   7   8   9   +

Pleasure: ○ ○ ○ ○ ○

Ingredients

Directions

Notes

Recipe

Prep Time:	Cook Time:	Difficulty: ○ ○ ○ ○ ○
Serves: 1 2 3 4 5 6 7 8 9 +		Pleasure: ○ ○ ○ ○ ○

Ingredients

Directions

Notes

Recipe

Prep Time:

Cook Time:

Difficulty: ○ ○ ○ ○ ○

Serves: 1 2 3 4 5 6 7 8 9 +

Pleasure: ○ ○ ○ ○ ○

D

Ingredients

Directions

Notes

Recipe

Prep Time: _____

Cook Time: _____

Difficulty: ○ ○ ○ ○ ○

Serves: 1   2   3   4   5   6   7   8   9   +

Pleasure: ○ ○ ○ ○ ○

Ingredients

_____   _____
_____   _____
_____   _____
_____   _____
_____   _____
_____   _____
_____   _____

Directions

_____
_____
_____
_____
_____
_____
_____
_____
_____
_____

Notes

_____
_____
_____
_____

Recipe

Prep Time:

Cook Time:

Difficulty: ○ ○ ○ ○ ○

Serves: 1   2   3   4   5   6   7   8   9   +

Pleasure: ○ ○ ○ ○ ○

D

Ingredients

Directions

Notes

Recipe

| Prep Time: | | Cook Time: | | Difficulty: ○ ○ ○ ○ ○ |

| Serves: 1 2 3 4 5 6 7 8 9 + | | Pleasure: ○ ○ ○ ○ ○ |

Ingredients

_____

_____

_____

_____

_____

_____

Directions

_____

_____

_____

_____

_____

_____

_____

_____

_____

Notes

_____

_____

_____

_____

A B C D E F G H I J K L M N O P Q R S T U V W X Y Z

Recipe

Prep Time:

Cook Time:

Difficulty: ○ ○ ○ ○ ○

Serves: 1   2   3   4   5   6   7   8   9   +

Pleasure: ○ ○ ○ ○ ○

Ingredients

Directions

Notes

Recipe

Prep Time:

Cook Time:

Difficulty: ○ ○ ○ ○ ○

Serves: 1 2 3 4 5 6 7 8 9 +

Pleasure: ○ ○ ○ ○ ○

Ingredients

Directions

Notes

Recipe

| Prep Time: | Cook Time: | Difficulty: ○ ○ ○ ○ ○ |

Serves: 1   2   3   4   5   6   7   8   9   +   Pleasure: ○ ○ ○ ○ ○

Ingredients

Directions

Notes

Recipe

Prep Time:

Cook Time:

Difficulty: ○ ○ ○ ○ ○

Serves: 1 2 3 4 5 6 7 8 9 +

Pleasure: ○ ○ ○ ○ ○

Ingredients

Directions

Notes

Recipe

Prep Time:	Cook Time:	Difficulty: ○ ○ ○ ○ ○

Serves: 1   2   3   4   5   6   7   8   9   +   Pleasure: ○ ○ ○ ○ ○

Ingredients

Directions

Notes

Recipe

Prep Time:

Cook Time:

Difficulty: ○ ○ ○ ○ ○

Serves: 1 2 3 4 5 6 7 8 9 +

Pleasure: ○ ○ ○ ○ ○

Ingredients

Directions

Notes

Recipe

Prep Time:

Cook Time:

Difficulty: ○ ○ ○ ○ ○

Serves: 1   2   3   4   5   6   7   8   9   +

Pleasure: ○ ○ ○ ○ ○

E

Ingredients

Directions

Notes

Recipe

Prep Time:

Cook Time:

Difficulty: ○ ○ ○ ○ ○

Serves: 1   2   3   4   5   6   7   8   9   +

Pleasure: ○ ○ ○ ○ ○

Ingredients

Directions

Notes

Recipe

Prep Time:

Cook Time:

Difficulty: ○ ○ ○ ○ ○

Serves: 1   2   3   4   5   6   7   8   9   +

Pleasure: ○ ○ ○ ○ ○

Ingredients

Directions

Notes

Recipe

Prep Time:	Cook Time:	Difficulty: ○ ○ ○ ○ ○

Serves: 1   2   3   4   5   6   7   8   9   +   Pleasure: ○ ○ ○ ○ ○

Ingredients

_____   _____
_____   _____
_____   _____
_____   _____
_____   _____
_____   _____
_____   _____

Directions

_____
_____
_____
_____
_____
_____
_____
_____
_____
_____
_____

Notes

_____
_____
_____
_____

Recipe

Prep Time:	Cook Time:	Difficulty: ○ ○ ○ ○ ○

Serves: 1   2   3   4   5   6   7   8   9   +   Pleasure: ○ ○ ○ ○ ○

Ingredients

Directions

Notes

Recipe

Prep Time:

Cook Time:

Difficulty: ○ ○ ○ ○ ○

Serves: 1 2 3 4 5 6 7 8 9 +

Pleasure: ○ ○ ○ ○ ○

Ingredients

Directions

Notes

Recipe

Prep Time:

Cook Time:

Difficulty: ○ ○ ○ ○ ○

Serves: 1   2   3   4   5   6   7   8   9   +

Pleasure: ○ ○ ○ ○ ○

Ingredients

Directions

Notes

Recipe

| Prep Time: | Cook Time: | Difficulty: ○ ○ ○ ○ ○ |

Serves: 1   2   3   4   5   6   7   8   9   +   Pleasure: ○ ○ ○ ○ ○

Ingredients

Directions

Notes

Recipe

Prep Time:	Cook Time:	Difficulty: ○ ○ ○ ○ ○
Serves: 1 2 3 4 5 6 7 8 9 +		Pleasure: ○ ○ ○ ○ ○

Ingredients

Directions

Notes

Recipe

Prep Time:

Cook Time:

Difficulty: ○ ○ ○ ○ ○

Serves: 1   2   3   4   5   6   7   8   9   +

Pleasure: ○ ○ ○ ○ ○

Ingredients

Directions

Notes

Recipe

Prep Time:

Cook Time:

Difficulty: ○ ○ ○ ○ ○

Serves: 1 2 3 4 5 6 7 8 9 +

Pleasure: ○ ○ ○ ○ ○

Ingredients

Directions

Notes

Recipe

Prep Time:

Cook Time:

Difficulty: ○ ○ ○ ○ ○

Serves: 1   2   3   4   5   6   7   8   9   +

Pleasure: ○ ○ ○ ○ ○

Ingredients

Directions

Notes

Recipe

Prep Time:

Cook Time:

Difficulty: ○ ○ ○ ○ ○

Serves: 1 2 3 4 5 6 7 8 9 +

Pleasure: ○ ○ ○ ○ ○

Ingredients

Directions

Notes

Recipe

Prep Time:	Cook Time:	Difficulty: ○ ○ ○ ○ ○

Serves: 1 2 3 4 5 6 7 8 9 +   Pleasure: ○ ○ ○ ○ ○

Ingredients

Directions

Notes

A B C D E F G H I J K L M N O P Q R S T U V W X Y Z

Recipe

Prep Time:

Cook Time:

Difficulty: ○ ○ ○ ○ ○

Serves: 1   2   3   4   5   6   7   8   9   +

Pleasure: ○ ○ ○ ○ ○

Ingredients

Directions

Notes

Recipe

| Prep Time: | Cook Time: | Difficulty: ○ ○ ○ ○ ○ |

Serves: 1   2   3   4   5   6   7   8   9   +   Pleasure: ○ ○ ○ ○ ○

Ingredients

Directions

Notes

Recipe

Prep Time:

Cook Time:

Difficulty: ○ ○ ○ ○ ○

Serves: 1   2   3   4   5   6   7   8   9   +

Pleasure: ○ ○ ○ ○ ○

Ingredients

H

Directions

Notes

Recipe

Prep Time:	Cook Time:	Difficulty: ○ ○ ○ ○ ○
Serves: 1 2 3 4 5 6 7 8 9 +		Pleasure: ○ ○ ○ ○ ○

Ingredients

_____   _____

_____   _____

_____   _____

_____   _____

_____   _____

_____   _____

_____   _____

Directions

_____

_____

_____

_____

_____

_____

_____

_____

_____

_____

_____

Notes

_____

_____

_____

_____

A
B
C
D
E
F
G
H
I
J
K
L
M
N
O
P
Q
R
S
T
U
V
W
X
Y
Z

Recipe

Prep Time:

Cook Time:

Difficulty: ○ ○ ○ ○ ○

Serves: 1   2   3   4   5   6   7   8   9   +

Pleasure: ○ ○ ○ ○ ○

Ingredients

Directions

Notes

Recipe

Prep Time:

Cook Time:

Difficulty: ○ ○ ○ ○ ○

Serves: 1   2   3   4   5   6   7   8   9   +

Pleasure: ○ ○ ○ ○ ○

Ingredients

Directions

Notes

Recipe

Prep Time: Cook Time: Difficulty: ○ ○ ○ ○ ○

Serves: 1   2   3   4   5   6   7   8   9   +   Pleasure: ○ ○ ○ ○ ○

Ingredients

Directions

Notes

Recipe

Prep Time:

Cook Time:

Difficulty: ○ ○ ○ ○ ○

Serves: 1   2   3   4   5   6   7   8   9   +

Pleasure: ○ ○ ○ ○ ○

Ingredients

Directions

Notes

A
B
C
D
E
F
G
H
I
J
K
L
M
N
O
P
Q
R
S
T
U
V
W
X
Y
Z

Recipe

Prep Time:

Cook Time:

Difficulty: ○ ○ ○ ○ ○

Serves: 1   2   3   4   5   6   7   8   9   +

Pleasure: ○ ○ ○ ○ ○

Ingredients

Directions

Notes

Recipe

Prep Time:	Cook Time:	Difficulty: ○ ○ ○ ○ ○

Serves: 1   2   3   4   5   6   7   8   9   +   Pleasure: ○ ○ ○ ○ ○

Ingredients

_____   _____

_____   _____

_____   _____

_____   _____

_____   _____

_____   _____

Directions

_____

_____

_____

_____

_____

_____

_____

_____

_____

_____

_____

Notes

_____

_____

_____

_____

A B C D E F G H I J K L M N O P Q R S T U V W X Y Z

Recipe

Prep Time:

Cook Time:

Difficulty: ○ ○ ○ ○ ○

Serves: 1   2   3   4   5   6   7   8   9   +

Pleasure: ○ ○ ○ ○ ○

Ingredients

Directions

Notes

Recipe

Prep Time:	Cook Time:	Difficulty: ○ ○ ○ ○ ○

Serves: 1   2   3   4   5   6   7   8   9   +   Pleasure: ○ ○ ○ ○ ○

Ingredients

Directions

Notes

Recipe

Prep Time:

Cook Time:

Difficulty: ○ ○ ○ ○ ○

Serves: 1   2   3   4   5   6   7   8   9   +

Pleasure: ○ ○ ○ ○ ○

Ingredients

Directions

Notes

Recipe

Prep Time:

Cook Time:

Difficulty: ○ ○ ○ ○ ○

Serves: 1 2 3 4 5 6 7 8 9 +

Pleasure: ○ ○ ○ ○ ○

Ingredients

Directions

Notes

Recipe

Prep Time:	Cook Time:	Difficulty: ○ ○ ○ ○ ○

Serves: 1 2 3 4 5 6 7 8 9 +	Pleasure: ○ ○ ○ ○ ○

Ingredients

Directions

Notes

J

Recipe

Prep Time:	Cook Time:	Difficulty: ○ ○ ○ ○ ○

Serves: 1 2 3 4 5 6 7 8 9 +	Pleasure: ○ ○ ○ ○ ○

Ingredients

_____   _____

_____   _____

_____   _____

_____   _____

_____   _____

Directions

_____

_____

_____

_____

_____

_____

_____

_____

_____

_____

Notes

_____

_____

_____

_____

A B C D E F G H I J K L M N O P Q R S T U V W X Y Z

Recipe

Prep Time:

Cook Time:

Difficulty: ○ ○ ○ ○ ○

Serves: 1 2 3 4 5 6 7 8 9 +

Pleasure: ○ ○ ○ ○ ○

Ingredients

Directions

Notes

J

Recipe

Prep Time:

Cook Time:

Difficulty: ○ ○ ○ ○ ○

Serves: 1 2 3 4 5 6 7 8 9 +

Pleasure: ○ ○ ○ ○ ○

Ingredients

Directions

Notes

Recipe

Prep Time:

Cook Time:

Difficulty: ○ ○ ○ ○ ○

Serves: 1 2 3 4 5 6 7 8 9 +

Pleasure: ○ ○ ○ ○ ○

Ingredients

_____   _____

_____   _____

_____   _____

_____   _____

_____   _____

_____   _____

K

Directions

_____

_____

_____

_____

_____

_____

_____

_____

_____

_____

_____

Notes

_____

_____

_____

_____

_____

Recipe

Prep Time:	Cook Time:	Difficulty: ○ ○ ○ ○ ○

Serves: 1 2 3 4 5 6 7 8 9 +	Pleasure: ○ ○ ○ ○ ○

Ingredients

Directions

Notes

A B C D E F G H I J K L M N O P Q R S T U V W X Y Z

Recipe

Prep Time:

Cook Time:

Difficulty: ○ ○ ○ ○ ○

Serves: 1 2 3 4 5 6 7 8 9 +

Pleasure: ○ ○ ○ ○ ○

Ingredients

K

Directions

Notes

Recipe

Prep Time:

Cook Time:

Difficulty: ○ ○ ○ ○ ○

Serves: 1 2 3 4 5 6 7 8 9 +

Pleasure: ○ ○ ○ ○ ○

Ingredients

Directions

A
B
C
D
E
F
G
H
I
J
K
L
M
N
O
P
Q
R
S
T
U
V
W
X
Y
Z

Notes

Recipe

Prep Time:

Cook Time:

Difficulty: ○ ○ ○ ○ ○

Serves: 1 2 3 4 5 6 7 8 9 +

Pleasure: ○ ○ ○ ○ ○

Ingredients

Directions

Notes

Recipe

Prep Time:

Cook Time:

Difficulty: ○ ○ ○ ○ ○

Serves: 1 2 3 4 5 6 7 8 9 +

Pleasure: ○ ○ ○ ○ ○

Ingredients

Directions

Notes

Recipe

Prep Time: | Cook Time: | Difficulty: ○ ○ ○ ○ ○

Serves: 1   2   3   4   5   6   7   8   9   + | Pleasure: ○ ○ ○ ○ ○

Ingredients

Directions

L

Notes

Recipe

Prep Time:

Cook Time:

Difficulty: ○ ○ ○ ○ ○

Serves: 1 2 3 4 5 6 7 8 9 +

Pleasure: ○ ○ ○ ○ ○

Ingredients

Directions

Notes

Recipe

Prep Time:	Cook Time:	Difficulty: ○ ○ ○ ○ ○

Serves: 1 2 3 4 5 6 7 8 9 +	Pleasure: ○ ○ ○ ○ ○

Ingredients

L

Directions

Notes

Recipe

Prep Time:

Cook Time:

Difficulty: ○ ○ ○ ○ ○

Serves: 1 2 3 4 5 6 7 8 9 +

Pleasure: ○ ○ ○ ○ ○

Ingredients

Directions

Notes

Recipe

Prep Time:	Cook Time:	Difficulty: ○ ○ ○ ○ ○
Serves: 1 2 3 4 5 6 7 8 9 +		Pleasure: ○ ○ ○ ○ ○

Ingredients

Directions

Notes

Recipe

Prep Time:	Cook Time:	Difficulty: ○ ○ ○ ○ ○

Serves: 1 2 3 4 5 6 7 8 9 +	Pleasure: ○ ○ ○ ○ ○

Ingredients

Directions

Notes

Recipe

Prep Time:

Cook Time:

Difficulty: ○ ○ ○ ○ ○

Serves: 1   2   3   4   5   6   7   8   9   +

Pleasure: ○ ○ ○ ○ ○

Ingredients

Directions

Notes

Recipe

Prep Time:		Cook Time:		Difficulty: ○ ○ ○ ○ ○

Serves: 1   2   3   4   5   6   7   8   9   +   Pleasure: ○ ○ ○ ○ ○

Ingredients

Directions

Notes

A
B
C
D
E
F
G
H
I
J
K
L
M
N
O
P
Q
R
S
T
U
V
W
X
Y
Z

Recipe

Prep Time:

Cook Time:

Difficulty: ○ ○ ○ ○ ○

Serves: 1   2   3   4   5   6   7   8   9   +

Pleasure: ○ ○ ○ ○ ○

Ingredients

Directions

Notes

Recipe

Prep Time:

Cook Time:

Difficulty: ○ ○ ○ ○ ○

Serves: 1   2   3   4   5   6   7   8   9   +

Pleasure: ○ ○ ○ ○ ○

Ingredients

Directions

Notes

Recipe

A
B
C
D
E
F
G
H
I
J
K
L
M
N
O
P
Q
R
S
T
U
V
W
X
Y
Z

Prep Time:

Cook Time:

Difficulty: ○ ○ ○ ○ ○

Serves: 1   2   3   4   5   6   7   8   9   +

Pleasure: ○ ○ ○ ○ ○

Ingredients

Directions

Notes

Recipe

| Prep Time: | Cook Time: | Difficulty: ○ ○ ○ ○ ○ |

| Serves: 1 2 3 4 5 6 7 8 9 + | Pleasure: ○ ○ ○ ○ ○ |

Ingredients

Directions

Notes

Recipe

Prep Time:	Cook Time:	Difficulty: ○ ○ ○ ○ ○
Serves: 1 2 3 4 5 6 7 8 9 +		Pleasure: ○ ○ ○ ○ ○

Ingredients

_____   _____

_____   _____

_____   _____

_____   _____

_____   _____

_____   _____

Directions

_____

_____

_____

_____

_____

_____

_____

_____

_____

_____

_____

Notes

_____

_____

_____

_____

Recipe

Prep Time:

Cook Time:

Difficulty: ○ ○ ○ ○ ○

Serves: 1 2 3 4 5 6 7 8 9 +

Pleasure: ○ ○ ○ ○ ○

Ingredients

Directions

Notes

Recipe

Prep Time:

Cook Time:

Difficulty: ○ ○ ○ ○ ○

Serves: 1   2   3   4   5   6   7   8   9   +

Pleasure: ○ ○ ○ ○ ○

Ingredients

Directions

Notes

Recipe

Prep Time:	Cook Time:	Difficulty: ○ ○ ○ ○ ○

Serves: 1   2   3   4   5   6   7   8   9   +   Pleasure: ○ ○ ○ ○ ○

Ingredients

_____   _____
_____   _____
_____   _____
_____   _____
_____   _____
_____   _____

Directions

_____
_____
_____
_____
_____
_____
_____
_____
_____

Notes

_____
_____
_____
_____

Recipe

Prep Time:

Cook Time:

Difficulty: ○ ○ ○ ○ ○

Serves: 1   2   3   4   5   6   7   8   9   +

Pleasure: ○ ○ ○ ○ ○

Ingredients

Directions

Notes

Recipe

| Prep Time: | Cook Time: | Difficulty: ○ ○ ○ ○ ○ |

Serves: 1   2   3   4   5   6   7   8   9   +   Pleasure: ○ ○ ○ ○ ○

Ingredients

_____   _____
_____   _____
_____   _____
_____   _____
_____   _____
_____   _____

Directions

_____
_____
_____
_____
_____
_____
_____
_____
_____

Notes

_____
_____
_____
_____

A
B
C
D
E
F
G
H
I
J
K
L
M
N
O
P
Q
R
S
T
U
V
W
X
Y
Z

Recipe

| Prep Time: | Cook Time: | Difficulty: ○ ○ ○ ○ ○ |

| Serves: 1 2 3 4 5 6 7 8 9 + | Pleasure: ○ ○ ○ ○ ○ |

Ingredients

Directions

Notes

Recipe

Prep Time:

Cook Time:

Difficulty: ○ ○ ○ ○ ○

Serves: 1 2 3 4 5 6 7 8 9 +

Pleasure: ○ ○ ○ ○ ○

Ingredients

Directions

Notes

A B C D E F G H I J K L M N O P Q R S T U V W X Y Z

Recipe

Prep Time:	Cook Time:	Difficulty: ○ ○ ○ ○ ○

Serves: 1 2 3 4 5 6 7 8 9 +   Pleasure: ○ ○ ○ ○ ○

Ingredients

_____   _____

_____   _____

_____   _____

_____   _____

_____   _____

_____   _____

Directions

_____

_____

_____

_____

_____

_____

_____

_____

_____

_____

Notes

_____

_____

_____

_____

Recipe

Prep Time:

Cook Time:

Difficulty: ○ ○ ○ ○ ○

Serves: 1 2 3 4 5 6 7 8 9 +

Pleasure: ○ ○ ○ ○ ○

Ingredients

Directions

Notes

Recipe

Prep Time: _____

Cook Time: _____

Difficulty: ○ ○ ○ ○ ○

Serves: 1 2 3 4 5 6 7 8 9 +

Pleasure: ○ ○ ○ ○ ○

Ingredients

_____
_____
_____
_____
_____
_____

_____
_____
_____
_____
_____
_____

Directions

_____
_____
_____
_____
_____
_____
_____
_____
_____
_____
_____
_____

Notes

_____
_____
_____
_____

Recipe

| Prep Time: | Cook Time: | Difficulty: ○ ○ ○ ○ ○ |

| Serves: 1   2   3   4   5   6   7   8   9   + | Pleasure: ○ ○ ○ ○ ○ |

Ingredients

Directions

O

| Notes |

Recipe

Prep Time:

Cook Time:

Difficulty: ○ ○ ○ ○ ○

Serves:　1　2　3　4　5　6　7　8　9　+

Pleasure: ○ ○ ○ ○ ○

Ingredients

Directions

P

Notes

Recipe

Prep Time:	Cook Time:	Difficulty: ○ ○ ○ ○ ○

Serves: 1   2   3   4   5   6   7   8   9   +   Pleasure: ○ ○ ○ ○ ○

Ingredients

_____   _____
_____   _____
_____   _____
_____   _____
_____   _____
_____   _____

Directions

_____
_____
_____
_____
_____
_____
_____
_____
_____

Notes

_____
_____
_____
_____

Recipe

Prep Time:

Cook Time:

Difficulty: ○ ○ ○ ○ ○

Serves: 1 2 3 4 5 6 7 8 9 +

Pleasure: ○ ○ ○ ○ ○

Ingredients

Directions

P

Notes

Recipe

Prep Time:	Cook Time:	Difficulty: ○ ○ ○ ○ ○

Serves: 1 2 3 4 5 6 7 8 9 +   Pleasure: ○ ○ ○ ○ ○

Ingredients

Directions

Notes

Recipe

Prep Time:

Cook Time:

Difficulty: ○ ○ ○ ○ ○

Serves: 1   2   3   4   5   6   7   8   9   +

Pleasure: ○ ○ ○ ○ ○

Ingredients

Directions

Notes

Recipe

| Prep Time: | Cook Time: | Difficulty: ○ ○ ○ ○ ○ |

| Serves: 1 2 3 4 5 6 7 8 9 + | Pleasure: ○ ○ ○ ○ ○ |

Ingredients

_____ _____
_____ _____
_____ _____
_____ _____
_____ _____
_____ _____

Directions

_____
_____
_____
_____
_____
_____
_____
_____
_____
_____

Notes

_____
_____
_____
_____

Recipe

Prep Time:	Cook Time:	Difficulty: ○ ○ ○ ○ ○

Serves: 1 2 3 4 5 6 7 8 9 +   Pleasure: ○ ○ ○ ○ ○

Ingredients

Directions

Notes

Recipe

Prep Time:

Cook Time:

Difficulty: ○ ○ ○ ○ ○

Serves: 1   2   3   4   5   6   7   8   9   +

Pleasure: ○ ○ ○ ○ ○

Ingredients

Directions

Notes

A B C D E F G H I J K L M N O P Q R S T U V W X Y Z

Recipe

Prep Time:

Cook Time:

Difficulty: ○ ○ ○ ○ ○

Serves: 1   2   3   4   5   6   7   8   9   +

Pleasure: ○ ○ ○ ○ ○

Ingredients

Directions

Notes

Recipe

Prep Time:	Cook Time:	Difficulty: ○ ○ ○ ○ ○

Serves: 1   2   3   4   5   6   7   8   9   +   Pleasure: ○ ○ ○ ○ ○

Ingredients

_____   _____

_____   _____

_____   _____

_____   _____

_____   _____

Directions

_____

_____

_____

_____

_____

_____

_____

_____

_____

Notes

A
B
C
D
E
F
G
H
I
J
K
L
M
N
O
P

Q

R
S
T
U
V
W
X
Y
Z

Recipe

Prep Time:

Cook Time:

Difficulty: ○ ○ ○ ○ ○

Serves: 1   2   3   4   5   6   7   8   9   +

Pleasure: ○ ○ ○ ○ ○

Ingredients

Directions

Notes

Recipe

Prep Time:

Cook Time:

Difficulty: ○ ○ ○ ○ ○

Serves: 1   2   3   4   5   6   7   8   9   +

Pleasure: ○ ○ ○ ○ ○

Ingredients

Directions

Q

Notes

A
B
C
D
E
F
G
H
I
J
K
L
M
N
O
P
R
S
T
U
V
W
X
Y
Z

Recipe

Prep Time:

Cook Time:

Difficulty: ○ ○ ○ ○ ○

Serves:　1　2　3　4　5　6　7　8　9　+

Pleasure: ○ ○ ○ ○ ○

Ingredients

Directions

Notes

Recipe

Prep Time: | Cook Time: | Difficulty: ○ ○ ○ ○ ○

Serves: 1   2   3   4   5   6   7   8   9   + | Pleasure: ○ ○ ○ ○ ○

Ingredients

Directions

R

Notes

Recipe

Prep Time:

Cook Time:

Difficulty: ○ ○ ○ ○ ○

Serves: 1   2   3   4   5   6   7   8   9   +

Pleasure: ○ ○ ○ ○ ○

Ingredients

Directions

R

Notes

Recipe

Prep Time:

Cook Time:

Difficulty: ○ ○ ○ ○ ○

Serves:　1　2　3　4　5　6　7　8　9　+

Pleasure: ○ ○ ○ ○ ○

Ingredients

Directions

R

Notes

Recipe

Prep Time:

Cook Time:

Difficulty: ○ ○ ○ ○ ○

Serves: 1   2   3   4   5   6   7   8   9   +

Pleasure: ○ ○ ○ ○ ○

Ingredients

Directions

R

Notes

Recipe

| Prep Time: | Cook Time: | Difficulty: ○ ○ ○ ○ ○ |

| Serves: 1   2   3   4   5   6   7   8   9   + | Pleasure: ○ ○ ○ ○ ○ |

Ingredients

_____   _____
_____   _____
_____   _____
_____   _____
_____   _____
_____   _____

Directions

_____
_____
_____
_____
_____
_____
_____
_____
_____
_____

Notes

_____
_____
_____
_____

Recipe

Prep Time:

Cook Time:

Difficulty: ○ ○ ○ ○ ○

Serves: 1   2   3   4   5   6   7   8   9   +

Pleasure: ○ ○ ○ ○ ○

Ingredients

Directions

S

Notes

Recipe

Prep Time:

Cook Time:

Difficulty: ○ ○ ○ ○ ○

Serves: 1   2   3   4   5   6   7   8   9   +

Pleasure: ○ ○ ○ ○ ○

Ingredients

Directions

Notes

Recipe

Prep Time:

Cook Time:

Difficulty: ○ ○ ○ ○ ○

Serves: 1 2 3 4 5 6 7 8 9 +

Pleasure: ○ ○ ○ ○ ○

Ingredients

Directions

Notes

Recipe

Prep Time:	Cook Time:	Difficulty: ○ ○ ○ ○ ○
Serves: 1 2 3 4 5 6 7 8 9 +		Pleasure: ○ ○ ○ ○ ○

Ingredients

_____   _____
_____   _____
_____   _____
_____   _____
_____   _____
_____   _____

Directions

_____
_____
_____
_____
_____
_____
_____
_____
_____
_____

Notes

_____
_____
_____
_____

A B C D E F G H I J K L M N O P Q R S T U V W X Y Z

Recipe

Prep Time:

Cook Time:

Difficulty: ○ ○ ○ ○ ○

Serves: 1 2 3 4 5 6 7 8 9 +

Pleasure: ○ ○ ○ ○ ○

Ingredients

Directions

A B C D E F G H I J K L M N O P Q R **S** T U V W X Y Z

Notes

Recipe

Prep Time:

Cook Time:

Difficulty: ○ ○ ○ ○ ○

Serves: 1   2   3   4   5   6   7   8   9   +

Pleasure: ○ ○ ○ ○ ○

Ingredients

Directions

Notes

Recipe

Prep Time:

Cook Time:

Difficulty: ○ ○ ○ ○ ○

Serves: 1   2   3   4   5   6   7   8   9   +

Pleasure: ○ ○ ○ ○ ○

Ingredients

Directions

Notes

Recipe _____

Prep Time:	Cook Time:	Difficulty: ○ ○ ○ ○ ○

Serves: 1 2 3 4 5 6 7 8 9 +	Pleasure: ○ ○ ○ ○ ○

Ingredients

_____ _____

_____ _____

_____ _____

_____ _____

_____ _____

_____ _____

Directions

_____

_____

_____

_____

_____

_____

_____

_____

_____

_____

Notes

_____

_____

_____

_____

Recipe

Prep Time:	Cook Time:	Difficulty: ○ ○ ○ ○ ○

Serves: 1 2 3 4 5 6 7 8 9 +	Pleasure: ○ ○ ○ ○ ○

Ingredients

Directions

T

Notes

Recipe

Prep Time:

Cook Time:

Difficulty: ○ ○ ○ ○ ○

Serves: 1   2   3   4   5   6   7   8   9   +

Pleasure: ○ ○ ○ ○ ○

Ingredients

Directions

Notes

A
B
C
D
E
F
G
H
I
J
K
L
M
N
O
P
Q
R
S
T
U
V
W
X
Y
Z

Recipe

| Prep Time: | Cook Time: | Difficulty: ○ ○ ○ ○ ○ |

Serves: 1   2   3   4   5   6   7   8   9   +   Pleasure: ○ ○ ○ ○ ○

Ingredients

_____   _____
_____   _____
_____   _____
_____   _____
_____   _____
_____   _____

Directions

_____
_____
_____
_____
_____
_____
_____
_____
_____
_____

Notes

_____
_____
_____
_____

A B C D E F G H I J K L M N O P Q R S T U V W X Y Z

Recipe

Prep Time:

Cook Time:

Difficulty: ○ ○ ○ ○ ○

Serves: 1 2 3 4 5 6 7 8 9 +

Pleasure: ○ ○ ○ ○ ○

Ingredients

Directions

Notes

A B C D E F G H I J K L M N O P Q R S T U V W X Y Z

Recipe

Prep Time:

Cook Time:

Difficulty: ○ ○ ○ ○ ○

Serves: 1 2 3 4 5 6 7 8 9 +

Pleasure: ○ ○ ○ ○ ○

Ingredients

Directions

U

Notes

Recipe

Prep Time:	Cook Time:	Difficulty: ○ ○ ○ ○ ○
Serves: 1 2 3 4 5 6 7 8 9 +		Pleasure: ○ ○ ○ ○ ○

Ingredients

Directions

Notes

A
B
C
D
E
F
G
H
I
J
K
L
M
N
O
P
Q
R
S
T
U
V
W
X
Y
Z

Recipe

Prep Time:

Cook Time:

Difficulty: ○ ○ ○ ○ ○

Serves: 1   2   3   4   5   6   7   8   9   +

Pleasure: ○ ○ ○ ○ ○

Ingredients

Directions

Notes

Recipe

Prep Time:

Cook Time:

Difficulty: ○ ○ ○ ○ ○

Serves: 1   2   3   4   5   6   7   8   9   +

Pleasure: ○ ○ ○ ○ ○

Ingredients

Directions

Notes

Recipe

Prep Time:	Cook Time:	Difficulty: ○ ○ ○ ○ ○

Serves: 1 2 3 4 5 6 7 8 9 +   Pleasure: ○ ○ ○ ○ ○

Ingredients

Directions

U

Notes

Recipe

Prep Time:

Cook Time:

Difficulty: ○ ○ ○ ○ ○

Serves: 1 2 3 4 5 6 7 8 9 +

Pleasure: ○ ○ ○ ○ ○

Ingredients

Directions

Notes

A
B
C
D
E
F
G
H
I
J
K
L
M
N
O
P
Q
R
S
T
U
V
W
X
Y
Z

Recipe

Prep Time:

Cook Time:

Difficulty: ○ ○ ○ ○ ○

Serves: 1   2   3   4   5   6   7   8   9   +

Pleasure: ○ ○ ○ ○ ○

Ingredients

Directions

Notes

Recipe

| Prep Time: | Cook Time: | Difficulty: ○ ○ ○ ○ ○ |

| Serves: 1   2   3   4   5   6   7   8   9   + | Pleasure: ○ ○ ○ ○ ○ |

Ingredients

Directions

Notes

A B C D E F G H I J K L M N O P Q R S T U V W X Y Z

Recipe

Prep Time:

Cook Time:

Difficulty: ○ ○ ○ ○ ○

Serves: 1 2 3 4 5 6 7 8 9 +

Pleasure: ○ ○ ○ ○ ○

Ingredients

Directions

V

Notes

Recipe

Prep Time:

Cook Time:

Difficulty: ○ ○ ○ ○ ○

Serves: 1   2   3   4   5   6   7   8   9   +

Pleasure: ○ ○ ○ ○ ○

Ingredients

Directions

Notes

A
B
C
D
E
F
G
H
I
J
K
L
M
N
O
P
Q
R
S
T
U
V
W
X
Y
Z

Recipe

Prep Time:

Cook Time:

Difficulty: ○ ○ ○ ○ ○

Serves: 1   2   3   4   5   6   7   8   9   +

Pleasure: ○ ○ ○ ○ ○

Ingredients

Directions

V

Notes

Recipe

Prep Time:

Cook Time:

Difficulty: ○ ○ ○ ○ ○

Serves: 1   2   3   4   5   6   7   8   9   +

Pleasure: ○ ○ ○ ○ ○

Ingredients

Directions

A B C D E F G H I J K L M N O P Q R S T U V W X Y Z

Notes

Recipe

Prep Time: | Cook Time: | Difficulty: ○ ○ ○ ○ ○

Serves: 1 2 3 4 5 6 7 8 9 + | Pleasure: ○ ○ ○ ○ ○

Ingredients

Directions

W

Notes

Recipe

Prep Time:

Cook Time:

Difficulty: ○ ○ ○ ○ ○

Serves: 1   2   3   4   5   6   7   8   9   +

Pleasure: ○ ○ ○ ○ ○

Ingredients

Directions

Notes

A
B
C
D
E
F
G
H
I
J
K
L
M
N
O
P
Q
R
S
T
U
V
W
X
Y
Z

Recipe

| Prep Time: | Cook Time: | Difficulty: ○ ○ ○ ○ ○ |

Serves: 1   2   3   4   5   6   7   8   9   +   Pleasure: ○ ○ ○ ○ ○

Ingredients

Directions

Notes

Recipe

Prep Time:	Cook Time:	Difficulty: ○ ○ ○ ○ ○

Serves: 1   2   3   4   5   6   7   8   9   +   Pleasure: ○ ○ ○ ○ ○

Ingredients

Directions

Notes

Recipe

Prep Time: | Cook Time: | Difficulty: ○ ○ ○ ○ ○

Serves: 1 2 3 4 5 6 7 8 9 + | Pleasure: ○ ○ ○ ○ ○

Ingredients

Directions

Notes

Recipe

Prep Time:	Cook Time:	Difficulty: ○ ○ ○ ○ ○

Serves: 1 2 3 4 5 6 7 8 9 +	Pleasure: ○ ○ ○ ○ ○

Ingredients

Directions

Notes

A
B
C
D
E
F
G
H
I
J
K
L
M
N
O
P
Q
R
S
T
U
V
W
X
Y
Z

Recipe

Prep Time:

Cook Time:

Difficulty: ○ ○ ○ ○ ○

Serves: 1 2 3 4 5 6 7 8 9 +

Pleasure: ○ ○ ○ ○ ○

Ingredients

Directions

Notes

Recipe

Prep Time:	Cook Time:	Difficulty: ○ ○ ○ ○ ○

Serves:　1　2　3　4　5　6　7　8　9　+　　Pleasure: ○ ○ ○ ○ ○

Ingredients

Directions

Notes

Recipe

Prep Time: | Cook Time: | Difficulty: ○ ○ ○ ○ ○

Serves: 1 2 3 4 5 6 7 8 9 + | Pleasure: ○ ○ ○ ○ ○

Ingredients

_____   _____
_____   _____
_____   _____
_____   _____
_____   _____
_____   _____

Directions

_____
_____
_____
_____
_____
_____
_____
_____
_____
_____
_____
_____

X

Notes

_____
_____
_____
_____

Recipe

Prep Time:

Cook Time:

Difficulty: ○ ○ ○ ○ ○

Serves:　1　2　3　4　5　6　7　8　9　+

Pleasure: ○ ○ ○ ○ ○

Ingredients

Directions

Notes

Recipe

Prep Time:

Cook Time:

Difficulty: ○ ○ ○ ○ ○

Serves: 1   2   3   4   5   6   7   8   9   +

Pleasure: ○ ○ ○ ○ ○

Ingredients

Directions

Notes

X

Recipe

Prep Time:

Cook Time:

Difficulty: ◯ ◯ ◯ ◯ ◯

Serves: 1   2   3   4   5   6   7   8   9   +

Pleasure: ◯ ◯ ◯ ◯ ◯

Ingredients

Directions

Notes

A
B
C
D
E
F
G
H
I
J
K
L
M
N
O
P
Q
R
S
T
U
V
W
X
Y
Z

Recipe

Prep Time:

Cook Time:

Difficulty: ○ ○ ○ ○ ○

Serves: 1 2 3 4 5 6 7 8 9 +

Pleasure: ○ ○ ○ ○ ○

Ingredients

Directions

Notes

A B C D E F G H I J K L M N O P Q R S T U V W X **Y** Z

Recipe

Prep Time:

Cook Time:

Difficulty: ○ ○ ○ ○ ○

Serves: 1   2   3   4   5   6   7   8   9   +

Pleasure: ○ ○ ○ ○ ○

Ingredients

Directions

Notes

Recipe

Prep Time:	Cook Time:	Difficulty: ○ ○ ○ ○ ○

Serves: 1   2   3   4   5   6   7   8   9   +   Pleasure: ○ ○ ○ ○ ○

Ingredients

Directions

Notes

Recipe

Prep Time:

Cook Time:

Difficulty: ○ ○ ○ ○ ○

Serves: 1 2 3 4 5 6 7 8 9 +

Pleasure: ○ ○ ○ ○ ○

Ingredients

Directions

Notes

A B C D E F G H I J K L M N O P Q R S T U V W X Y Z

Recipe

Prep Time:

Cook Time:

Difficulty: ○ ○ ○ ○ ○

Serves: 1 2 3 4 5 6 7 8 9 +

Pleasure: ○ ○ ○ ○ ○

Ingredients

Directions

Notes

A
B
C
D
E
F
G
H
I
J
K
L
M
N
O
P
Q
R
S
T
U
V
W
X
Y
Z

Recipe

Prep Time:	Cook Time:	Difficulty: ○ ○ ○ ○ ○

Serves:　1　2　3　4　5　6　7　8　9　+

Pleasure: ○ ○ ○ ○ ○

Ingredients

_____   _____
_____   _____
_____   _____
_____   _____
_____   _____
_____   _____

Directions

_____
_____
_____
_____
_____
_____
_____
_____
_____
_____
_____

Notes

_____
_____
_____

A
B
C
D
E
F
G
H
I
J
K
L
M
N
O
P
Q
R
S
T
U
V
W
X
Y
Z

Recipe

Prep Time:

Cook Time:

Difficulty: ○ ○ ○ ○ ○

Serves: 1   2   3   4   5   6   7   8   9   +

Pleasure: ○ ○ ○ ○ ○

Ingredients

Directions

Notes

Recipe

Prep Time:	Cook Time:	Difficulty: ○ ○ ○ ○ ○

Serves: 1   2   3   4   5   6   7   8   9   +   Pleasure: ○ ○ ○ ○ ○

Ingredients

Directions

Notes

Recipe

Prep Time:	Cook Time:	Difficulty: ○ ○ ○ ○ ○

Serves: 1 2 3 4 5 6 7 8 9 +   Pleasure: ○ ○ ○ ○ ○

Ingredients

_____ _____

_____ _____

_____ _____

_____ _____

_____ _____

_____ _____

Directions

_____

_____

_____

_____

_____

_____

_____

_____

_____

_____

_____

Notes

_____

_____

_____

_____

A B C D E F G H I J K L M N O P Q R S T U V W X Y **Z**

Recipe

Prep Time:

Cook Time:

Difficulty: ○ ○ ○ ○ ○

Serves: 1 2 3 4 5 6 7 8 9 +

Pleasure: ○ ○ ○ ○ ○

Ingredients

Directions

Notes

A B C D E F G H I J K L M N O P Q R S T U V W X Y Z

Recipe

Prep Time:

Cook Time:

Difficulty: ○ ○ ○ ○ ○

Serves: 1   2   3   4   5   6   7   8   9   +

Pleasure: ○ ○ ○ ○ ○

Ingredients

Directions

Notes

Z

Recipe

Prep Time:

Cook Time:

Difficulty: ○ ○ ○ ○ ○

Serves: 1   2   3   4   5   6   7   8   9   +

Pleasure: ○ ○ ○ ○ ○

Ingredients

Directions

Notes

Made in the USA
Columbia, SC
20 November 2023